Dark spaces

Dark spaces

Mirna Grlj

To order additional copies of this book, contact:
Xlibris
1-800-455-039
www.Xlibris.com.au
Orders@Xlibris.com.au
795450

Contents

The Beginning

en years, a decade—that's how long I have been battling a side effect so horrendous in its form that I began to seek answers as to why it was happening. I remember life before it; there has to be a reason why it started happening. Dizzy spell, manic episode, or whatever I called it, I wanted to know why it was there, so I began to search. When did this start? What was different in my life or new when it started? When did Alice fall down the rabbit hole?

Before this disaster, I was after help, a way out, an escape, you could say, from the crippling anxiety. So, let us go back to the beginning. When I was a child, my parents saw me as the quiet, obedient, and calm child, and I was, but there was more to it. Fear. Fear of things that didn't quite make sense but it was clear as day that I was an anxious child— anxious about sound, light, images, people, events. Almost everything seemed overwhelming. My parents kept me home instead of sending me to day care; they sent my siblings off to day care but kept the quiet and calm one home. I didn't give them trouble, I suppose, so why would they need to send me off for the day? But to me, I believe that was the initial mistake. I sat in front of the TV for periods of time, played with my dolls, and quietly sat around as a child. That, to my mother, was such a relief, and she took comfort in my placid nature, not knowing that a lot of the time it was actually fear or empathy. Even as a very young child, not even five, I empathised with things that most children would just shrug off. I cried a lot when watching cartoons or movies, as scenes where animals passed away or ran off made me roll over in tears and I would cry over sad songs that none of my siblings even noticed were playing. It was clear; it was true—I was a highly sensitive child that grew into an empathetic adult with many years of suffering with high-functioning anxiety and obsessive thinking. My signs were missed or mistaken for good behaviour, but it was so much more than that.

When I hit my teenage years, I found myself searching the Internet for anxiety medication. Back then, medication for anxiety seemed taboo to my family as well as me, but I was on a mission to get it and understand it. The first psychiatrist I saw was very quick to open his little cabinet of magic and prescribe me fluvoxamine, the first SSRI I was on. Since starting my first ever SSRI, my early teenage years became a blur, a rough sketch of medication, weight loss, and side effects. Let me tell this part in detail, well, I don't know about detail but let me try and not miss the important and interesting bits. When I started my first SSRI, fluvoxamine, my life took a huge turn, actually, no, a 360. I just changed. I was no longer, well, you know, shy or held back. All of a sudden, things I usually would not do, I did; it was like puberty and SSRIs kicked in all at once, and it was like a slap in the face. When I started the SSRI, I was excited. Yes, how exciting, I am about to take the magic pills I have wanted for a while now, and it will all get better and we will never speak of anxiety again. We will never know of it or be bothered by it. I will go on to sleep well, live well, and just be well—how exciting is that, right? No, not quite, Mirna, it doesn't actually work that way, and it didn't. Yes, I started to sleep, and that felt amazing, I was sleeping, I was actually sleeping facing whatever side I want. I say that because before the SSRI, for years and years, I slept facing the open space, slightly tilting my head towards the ground because that was the only way I could sleep. I was too petrified to have my back to the open room. I would get such bad neck pain and shoulder pain; my arms would even go numb, but I did not move, not if I wanted some sleep. I wanted sleep so much; for years, all I wanted was sleep, but anxiety wouldn't let me, OCD (Obsessive Compulsive Disorders) wouldn't let me, and if it did, it wasn't comfortably. Bit off track now let's go back to the SSRIs being the answer to my problems. They were, yet they weren't. Well, they were until the side effect kicked in. I won't go into detail about high school; that is best left in the past. I'm not fond of the years, although they have been valuable lessons. At the start of high school, I wasn't the most popular—not that I cared, because being popular meant being the opposite of what I stand for. I was looked at as weird, different, and I was just unwanted by so many. I remember getting off the school bus in the afternoons, and one of my peers would start clapping and cheering. I went off, and other peers would join in on clapping. It sounded like a round of applause, yet it wasn't quite that; it felt horrible and embarrassing. Embarrassed of what exactly? I don't know, but I did not enjoy being cheered off the bus. In my later years of high school, there was a lot that went on, and a lot of it was due to that manic side effect and I'd really rather not go there; some of it was not the manic side effect, rather me acting on impulse and highs. Everyone has probably moved on by now. It has been over a decade, but for me, it haunts me to this day, and I still see that time of my life in my dreams; it all has become a reoccurring dream. I believe this is happening because I so much regret how I went about my last two years in high school and I am sorry for the hearts I broke and friendships I ruined because of my OCD and distorted thinking, I wish I knew then that it was OCD and got the help I needed and changed it all. This is probably nothing to most people and just a normal part of high school, although I don't look at it that way because when you have OCD, everything is done a bit differently and it can affect people and yourself. Then years later as you get older and wiser, you look back at it all through a magnifying glass and you realise how you behaved and just cry in regret. In case you are thinking, 'Well, what is it? What do you mean?' Well, one thing I used to do was isolate myself from my peers every recess and lunch. I would sit in the art room waiting for the boy I liked to show up or just sit in the corridors with another student or by myself, doing nothing. Missing out on friendships, laughter, and the fun of the playground and for what? This happened for many years, and it is sad and I do regret it although I try not to and to accept it and move on. I do feel sorry for myself, so sorry that I still cry because I so badly want to have done it differently and then things might have been completely different. I will keep it all in the corridors of my mind that nobody can walk through but me.

I will say though my visual arts teachers in year eleven and twelve will be forever etched in my mind. I feel they understood some parts of me and they helped shape who I am today and the interests I now have; I hope they know it. I find myself writing and then pressing the backspace bar a lot. Stay on track, Mirna. So yes, I wanted to be like my art teachers, an art teacher. While everyone from high school was going on to have babies or a degree, I was off to learn and study art. I enrolled in a diploma of fine arts in hope of completing that and then continuing to study for a teaching degree and then voila, I am an art teacher. Oh, also an English teacher—really wanted to teach that as well. All that did not happen, not in that order, kind of not at all. Am I making sense? Okay, I'll explain: I went on to complete my diploma of fine arts, then I went on to start a bachelor of teaching and lasted basically a semester before I fell apart. Art school—let's call it art school—was so interesting. I started art school at eighteen, so young, so naive yet such a thinker, and completed it just before I turned twenty. I met extraordinary people, a couple of whom I am close with today and mean a lot to me. I majored in photography; this was so cathartic, a huge contribution to my state of mind. Photography was so much more than an art form; for me, it was reality, therapy, and a form of communication. One of my works that was based on anxiety and mental health was placed in the end-of-year art school exhibition; it was sold and I was thrilled, yet the moment I actually sold it was taken from me by that terrible thief of a side effect. When the buyer came to collect the artwork, the side effect hit me; all that I wanted to say and could have said was gone and it was too late. The buyer came; I answered the door. I was physically there, but mentally, I was gone. Looking back at it now, it makes me so upset. I quickly gave the artwork to the buyer, said thank you, and was ready to go back inside until the buyer asked me to sign it first. Oops, yes, okay, I signed it and gave it to the buyer, and off I went back inside, like nothing ever happened. Mirna! Looking back now, I wanted so much to have explained the work and expressed how happy I was for the buyer to have chosen my work. The buyer told me that this work was for their daughter who gets butterflies in her stomach. The work was of an X-ray with butterflies in the stomach, and this work was a visual representation to help their daughter understand that feeling and perhaps not feel so alone. That work is somewhere in this world, hanging on a wall or placed on a shelf, and I long so much to know who that buyer was and where they are so I can explain it all and make a much better impression. That's okay; it is done now, and I will try and accept it and keep going. I just hope it is helping someone feel less alone.

This side effect made me so strange I just could not understand it; I once bought a pair of shoes that light up because of it and a pair of expensive boots that I usually would not buy in my normal state of mind. It was like full-blown mania, buying unusual things, saying unusual things, and thinking I was invincible at times as well. Interesting how I felt invincible when I also felt like I was dying. Was I high? Was this what this was? Either my body just couldn't handle the dose of serotonin I was on, causing mania, or I would just be high from it. I don't know. I say high because even though it was a terrible side effect, it did feel good at times, like I was flying or spinning, such an out-of-this-world feeling. I wasn't myself; whatever it was, it took me away from me.

A particular memory in my mind revisits me often, almost haunting me. I remember in painting or drawing class once, that side effect hit me and I ended up curled in foetal position on the floor in the middle of the class. At the time, I had no care or shame, and I just wanted to curl up on the floor with a heap of saliva accumulating in my mouth. My photography teacher may have been visiting the class at the time because I remember him being there, kneeling down next to me, asking me if I was okay and to try going outside for some air. I wasn't really responding; I just remember not wanting to move and maybe saying a couple of words like 'I'm okay' and everyone looking at me with expressionless faces, not knowing what to do and what was happening to me. Then soon after, the embarrassment showed up and I started to regret it all, and I just wanted it to never happen again. But it did, again and again and again. At the train station, on my way home from college, it hit me, and I put my head down and started to look unwell on a bench on the platform. People started to notice, and one person came over, asking if I was okay and if I needed an ambulance. I looked up all drowsy and barely able to put my head up and tell them, 'I'm okay, thank you.' For some reason, the feeling was like some sort of high maybe, like euphoria yet unpleasant in a way. I struggle to find the words to explain it. My family knew when it hit, and I didn't like that because I don't want them to know. I don't want anybody to know because I don't like to upset them. They say they can tell from my eyes; my eyes drop, they would say, and I found that hard to understand. In time, I came to understand it.

At times, I find myself questioning everything and where I am today. Is it all part of the mania? It is all one big side effect? Is where I am today a result of the choices I made when I was having that manic side effect? What a scary thought that is. How many hearts have I broken and how much time have I wasted if it all is? Yet I believe the questioning is part of this whole disorder; the ruminating and obsessive thinking is just a part of it all, unfortunately.

Once I graduated from college, I went on to enrol in university in hope of being a high school English and art teacher. I didn't. I didn't even get through the first year of university without falling apart; for some reason, it just was all too much, and it wasn't making sense to me. Doing university now, though, is such a different ball game. One semester into university, and I was already in the councillor's office pouring my heart out and spilling all my thoughts. I withdrew from university shortly after seeing the councillor. I was also juggling work and dating; it all got too much. The dating was also a secret, and it made it even harder to get by. I am now happily married to him though, and I have overcome that hurdle. For my first assignment at university, I remember failing. I even remember the mark, and I also remember crying once I received it. When I left university, I left past the census date, meaning I had fees looming over me that I simply could not afford or did not want to tell my family about. My mental health was not in the best state at the time, and I was able to gather medical certificates and documents to support me and did not have to pay any penalties or fees, thank goodness for the years of mental health records.

I was working in retail while at university and I continued to work in retail until I discovered administration. I was a job seeker for many months until I found a job in retail. I enjoyed it until the side effect hit me; we are calling it the side effect because I really don't know what else to call it. During a shift, the side effect hit me like a tidal wave, and I needed to sit down. I needed to get away, so I went and sat in the storage room. I may have sat there for ten minutes or so because the store manager who was working with me at the time came looking for me. It only felt like a few seconds, but it must have been a lot longer for the manager to come looking for me. My head was down, and I was sitting in the storeroom when the manger came in; she looked at me and right away asked me if I was okay or what was wrong. It was all a blur. I don't remember it much, but I do remember being so embarrassed and upset and almost in tears, saying, 'I need the money, please' because I got sent home and I was worried I would not get paid. Now I would never say anything like that, but when the side effect hits, I have no filter and I just say anything that comes to my mind. The manager was very understanding and did not seem upset with me at all.

I did enjoy retail, but it didn't last long because I soon ventured into the office world. I felt a bit lost once I left university and when I left retail, so I enrolled into an administration course at TAFE. I really put my mind into the course because I wanted to take on more responsibility and feel that I have earned something that I worked for. Towards the end of my course, I started looking for work in administration and came across a traineeship position. I loved the idea of working and earning, and not just money but a qualification. So, once I completed TAFE, I went on to do the traineeship and work full-time. The traineeship was in the field of administration, and I would be working as a recruiter at the same time—funny how I was the job seeker then ended up as the recruiter. It went so fast, and from there, I wanted to continue to venture through the office world, so I went on to work as an assistant recruiter and I was excited. I was actually very keen to continue on this path. I felt a sense of accomplishment: here I was in this position so close to the harbour and a really nice gym across the road that I joined and went to on my lunch breaks and then comfortably back to work. That feeling did not last long. I lost the job; the position was made redundant, and I was upset and felt confused, yet it was meant to be that way, so I accepted it.

When I lost the job, I rang my mother, crying. I felt like a failure, and Mum was so comforting and assured me things that would be okay and this was life and not to worry. Mum gave me a sense of hope and relief. I am so thankful for having her. This job in particular I lost because of dystonia—well, they didn't say that. I was told I was being made redundant as this was the first time it existed and it had not worked out, so I was made redundant.

The lead-up to me losing my job was me feeling nauseous roughly a week prior to losing this job and visited a medical centre. I was prescribed a medication for nausea that most people probably are fine with, but for me, my whole body rejected it. All of a sudden, soon after taking it, I struggled to breathe and began to lose control of my limbs. I had this urge to kick my legs or walk, my arms were curling in, and my mouth was drooping to one side as if I was having a stroke; it was absolutely shock horror. My dad took me to the emergency room at the hospital, and I ran in straight to the reception area and asked for help. I was in such a panic that I remember begging for help, not sure what kind of help; at this stage, I just did not want to die. I stayed at the hospital for hours. They knew I have anxiety; there is a record of it in their database. But this time it was not anxiety; this was something else. After running tests and having my dad sit with me for hours looking as pale as a ghost, nothing came up in the tests, nothing alarming. When my blood pressure was being taken,

I remember my arm curling in and crying with confusion. I felt lost and confused. The nurses looked puzzled. Someone from the mental health sector came to see me as well—could have been a nurse or a psychologist, I don't know. I remember being called in, given a bed, and asked questions. I can't even remember the questions. I just remember rolling on the bed in discomfort and gasping for air. I would sit up then lie down, sit up and lie down, trying to breathe and keep my body still. I just couldn't control my legs. After I received the all clear with the results, I went home, not feeling any better yet. I went home and took the medication again the next day just before heading to work, as I was still feeling nauseous. I went to work with out-of-control legs, anxiety, and not being able to sit still. Soon after arriving at work, I could not sit at my desk; my legs would keep kicking and having spasms. I was about to cry, and I got up and told my colleague I was going for a walk, sounding like I was about to cry; I clearly remember the look of confusion on her face. I walked the streets of the busy city as I held back my tears; the rest of the day was a blur. Soon after that day, I was called into a room and told I was being made redundant. My boss knew of my anxiety and seemed supportive, but this was something different. I spent some time at home the following day, and as I lay in my bed at home, I felt like I was falling, like I was falling through the bed, as if some black hole opened up and sucked me through. I would get up each time I felt that way.

I did not eat much at all or even move from my bed. I looked frail and drained. Anyone who came to visit me or looked at me that day seemed frightened and confused. When all of this came to pass, I was back at job seeking. I found a position in administration, and this time, it was being a receptionist for a chartered accountant's company. During this time, it was very close to my wedding, and I wanted to save money and pay for what I could. I wanted to show my parents that I could help them and I was not co-dependent. I wanted my parents to relax and not have all the costs on them. It also felt rewarding to work and earn then pay for my things. Probation can be six months in a position, and that felt unsettling and awfully long; it's like holding your breath for six months in fear of this and that. So, in case you are waiting for it, I will let you know I did lose that position as well, right before my wedding. I was upset. I was this and I was that, and like the usual, I accepted and moved on.

How can I forget this part? Just before I lost the job, I enrolled into a certificate three in early childhood education. I took the leap and headed in that direction. Are you wondering where the interest in childcare came from? To go straight to the point, it was when my nieces and nephew came along, and a huge part of my world changed. I enjoyed being around them so much; I wanted to always see them grow and learn, and I really enjoyed it. And by now, I had enough of adults and the adults' corporate world; it just seemed so toxic and numbers driven. I wanted out. I feel I gave the corporate world my all, and it seemed it wasn't good enough. And in this last office position, I really was not a fan of cleaning all the accountants' and lawyer's dishes. Seriously, people, how can that be part of a receptionist's job description? Might as well be spoon-feeding them all as they attend to their work. During the last office position just before they let me go, I was crying often; something came over me like bouts of depression, and I just could not hold back my tears and emotions. One of my colleagues would notice me crying, and although they were asking if I was okay, they also seemed confused because soon after my depressive episodes, I was called into the office and spoken to by one of my managers and let go. The timing was interesting; it seemed like such a cutthroat emotionless industry. Just do your job and show no emotion or feeling of any sort, or goodbye—that's how it felt for me. When I was enrolling into childcare study, I was nervous and full of questions and what-ifs; it did not stop me, though. I had a feeling that it would be okay and that it was the anxiety talking. I was in the elevator at the time and I wanted nobody to hear me so I wouldn't lose my job. Once I enrolled, I looked forward to the new beginning.

Soon after I lost this last job, I went on to get married. I married into a world that could not be any more different from the world I was brought up in, yet in time, a lot of it didn't seem different at all. Once I returned from the honeymoon, I commenced study. I really was focused on my study and had my eyes set on the goal. I wanted this. I wanted to graduate and enter this career path. During the study, I came across the practicum units where I was required to do work at an early childhood centre while studying. I contacted several early learning centres, and when one accepted me as a practicum student, I was excited and soon began. I fulfilled my practicum student duties and highly enjoyed it. I got offered casual work at this centre, and I was absolutely thrilled to jump on board. I started working casually, and it was amazing; I enjoyed it and was soon offered a permanent position within the same company but different centre just several streets away. When I first started as a permanent employee, I was in a completely different environment from where I worked casually, different in so many ways, and that scared me and had me wondering what on earth was in store for me. In time, it got easier, and I became very familiar with the environment that I stayed there for roughly four years; overall, I was with the company for around five years if you add up my casual work. That side effect hit me in this job, but not often at all. I came to notice the side effect was beginning to come over me at night. If it was to come over me, I preferred it to happen at night, away from the world, away from the eyes of many. I did not like people knowing about it or seeing it. I was uncomfortable about it and didn't want it to be a part of my identity. Unfortunately, I don't think it really mattered what I wanted; it was there, happening. This side effect was brought on several ways. It seemed to have its triggers; there were things that woke the beast from its slumber: caffeine, medication, chemicals.

That one particular side effect that had a hold of me for most of my teenage years and well into my early adulthood consumed me, and it consumed me whole. It hit me by surprise; when things were okay, there it was, ready to swallow me whole. I began to grow sick of this manic-like side effect that had me impulsive, out of the ordinary, sweating, heart racing and biting myself to the bone. I spent a lot of time going back and forth between GPs, trying to explain this side effect, trying to make sense of it. As good as my doctors were, they struggled to understand what exactly was happening to me. They looked puzzled and almost in doubt that they even believed what was happening to me. My family was just as confused, especially my husband. Low iron, fatigue, or simply not drinking enough water were all things thrown at me by my family to try and explain it all. I knew deep down that none of these was the case; it was the medication somehow doing this to me, but I had no way of proving my theory. After years of suffering and complaining, I was referred by my doctor to my second psychiatrist. I saw the hope in the doctor's eyes that this would once and for all help me find peace.

My oh my, will I be forever grateful for meeting the second psychiatrist who diagnosed the OCD and explained it all for me. Since I was so certain of what was causing the side effect, I explained it, and right away, we were on the same page. At the end of my first appointment, we came to a conclusion, which is also the solution now: to compound the medication, getting it made into a lower dosage. The lowest dose of the medication available is 30 mg, and anything lower requires compounding. So, the psychiatrist wrote me a script that stated for the medication to me compounded to 5 mg pills; this way, I could slowly drop by five to eventually find the right dose for me. For the first time round, I gradually dropped from 30 mg to 25 mg and stayed on that dose for roughly two months to see if the side effect went away. It didn't, and what came along was even worse. What was ahead was a daunting ride.

The Change

So, I had known for many years what was happening to me was caused by the anxiety medication, but I just had no way of naming it and explaining it in scientific terms or in a way that made sense to the doctors or anyone. The psychiatrist explained it and put it all in a simple yet very important explanation. I am most likely a slow metaboliser of drugs, such as antidepressants; therefore, taking it at even the smallest dose makes me go through the side effect. It could possibly be medication-induced mania. Bingo! There it was, a proper explanation finally we could see clearly! There it was! This might be the reason! Oh, I just wanted to shout it from the rooftops and let everybody know what I had been trying to explain all these years. So I asked the psychiatrist 'Why haven't any of the doctors I have seen all these years figured this out, and you figured it out within an hour of seeing me for the first time?' He simply answered, 'Ask them.' With a giggle of relief and hope, we moved on, and he went through explaining to me how to get the medication compounded and how it would work. To put it simply, being a slow metaboliser of chemicals or drugs such as antidepressants, alcohol, and caffeine means what most people can handle, I cannot handle. Even the minimum sold is too strong for me. My body metabolises the chemicals slowly; therefore, these build up fairly quickly in my system and become toxic and therefore cause strange side effects almost every day. Although this was not proven or confirmed by a test, it was likely true, as I ticked all the boxes for being a slow metaboliser; it made sense. Oh, the bittersweet relief of getting this explained and getting the medication compounded—it gave me so much hope. So here it is, the horrible part. It wasn't easy cutting down medication to the dose suitable for me, having the medication compounded into five-milligram capsules allowed me to drop slowly by fives until I found the right dose for me, for my metabolic rate. The torture? The outburst and bouts of gastro-oesophageal reflux. It had me skating on thin ice, and oh, did I feel like I was going to break and I would give up and go back to the full dose that's not right for me but easier to be on. But I didn't, I stuck through roughly two months of reflux up to my ears, literally, and even my nose. Everything made its way up my oesophagus like a violent volcano erupting and wiping out all in its path. I was adamant that this indeed would pass, that this was withdrawal symptoms, and so I held my breath when I had the reflux, and it all subsided in two months. My body adapted. My body accepted and got used to the 25 mg. Now as the side effects were still happening plus the reflux, I couldn't do much about it until my second appointment. It seemed like a very long two months, but I made it.

During my second appointment, I explained to the psychiatrist that I had horrible reflux, but it did subside. I also told him that the side effect was still there, so we agreed to drop the dose by another 5 mg so I would be on 20 mg. I had to try that for another month and then see him again to monitor the result. The 20 mg got rid of the side effect but welcomed back my anxiety. In the early hours of the morning, I suffered terrors and nightmares. When the morning came, it brought fear, along with it my childhood fears. This was bothersome, yet what a relief that after all these years, this side effect is rarely showing its face now. I went from having it several times a week or so to having it once every few months. I feel I have won a part of my life back; it is so exciting that I am writing about it now. It finally leaves me alone most of the time. I don't know when it will appear again. I am just enjoying all the days without it. I feel free.

It's amazing how your body reacts to anxiety as if it is under attack. I picked out a blouse and put it on; it was a cold winter's day, yet I knew that in time after moving around and running errands, my body would heat up, and I would become hot. So I went on without a jacket; the blouse was long-sleeved, so it wasn't too bad. I was a bit cold, but I still managed to sweat up a storm. I could feel the sweat seeping through my pores in many areas of my body but not because of the weather, no. I was sweating from a rush of anxiety, a rush of thoughts that sent my body into emergency defence mode. I thought, oh, a top I wore once needed to be washed after half hour of driving and an hour of shopping, fantastic. But I'm used to this; much of my top-half clothing can only be worn once because being in a state of panic often causes me to perspire a lot over nothing.

Almost forgot to mention when that side effect hit, I would also have problems going to the toilet, as if my bladder stopped working. I would be busting to go toilet and I would sit on the toilet and try to go, but it would not come out. I just could not urinate. What was going on? What was this? I still don't know, but it could be due to the anxiety or another physical symptom of this side effect of being a slow metaboliser. It feels so uncomfortable not being able to go toilet when you really need to; having urine sit there and not pass gave me this dull pressure in my bladder or surrounding area. It was so unpleasant. Once the side effect passes, I am able to go toilet, and when I do, I continue to go over and over, as if the ocean filled up inside within the few hours that I was not well. The time between each toilet trip felt like hours when it wasn't at all. Because I know what brings on this side effect, I am very cautious as to what I have or how much of it I have. I love coffee, and unfortunately, caffeine is one of the main contributors to this side effect. I can still have it; it just has to be weak. I ask for a half-strength cappuccino, and that won't affect me; it just has to be a weak coffee because a standard cup that most people probably drink is like having a double shot of caffeine or more in one cup for me. Half strength is enough for me and works wonders; even decaf works for me. For a while, before I was aware I am a slow metaboliser, I was drinking a full-strength standard cup of coffee, and that was when I would fall into this side effect often, not knowing it was the coffee.

OCD manifests in many ways; when I thought I was free of one obsession, I'd feel such relief until another one arose. OCD never really leaves you or just stops. It just changes form; it finds things you are sensitive towards and torments you with those. My obsessions ranged from sexuality, body image, certain people, relationships, horror movies, and so much more, I feel I could go on forever. I feel a sense of shame and discomfort about going into detail about these obsessions, although I feel I should. Horror movies were my earliest and longest for OCD and still are; they kept me up most nights for years. I would sleep with the lights on; whether kitchen light, bathroom light, or corridor light, a light had to be on. I would ask Mum or my sister to sleep next to me, and I even had a certain way of sleeping: I had to always see the floor.

It is only recently I began to realise that the horror movie images in my head on repeat are OCD; most of my life I just thought it was anxiety. I did not know much about OCD growing up, and no doctor or therapist told me what it was. I feel I had to diagnose myself, then the doctors agreed and approved it! Not the other way around, the way I would have liked it to be to save me all the headache or searching! I never watched a horror movie in full; it was always snippets, scenes that would catch my eye or the scary noises I would hear from the TV when I was in another room. That was enough for it to petrify me and stick in my mind like a leech sucking the life out of me. My siblings were complete opposites to me; they loved to watch horror movies, and although I would cry when they decided to watch them, they still did and I would just have to leave the room or the house. Any scene that I saw even by accident would repeat like a CD stuck on repeat and nobody stepping in to press Stop. Characters' faces from the horror movies and certain scenes were constantly playing in my mind for days, weeks, and now years. So much pain and suffering has been brought on because of this horror movie OCD; it made me feel so detached from the world. Sleeping, eating, showering, going to school or work, and the ability to do things by myself were all taken from me for so many years, thinking about it and writing about it makes me want to fall to the floor and cry.

The sexuality OCD I do not want to go into much detail about. I will leave you to do the research and see for yourselves. A bit about it is that I would obsess about my sexual orientation, other people sexually, infidelity, and relationships. It was like I did not know who I was, and I was so afraid of hurting others and myself emotionally. I would obsess about certain people to the point I would dream about them; it actually would drive me mad.

When OCD starts to involve other people, things become even scarier, next-level scary. Like OCD about contamination, mothers with OCD may fear that they have not washed their child's bottle enough times before giving it to the child and their child will get very sick, so they stay up at night constantly checking their child's breathing, heart rate, or pulse. Contamination OCD can be time-consuming; I would spend up to half an hour washing my hands or body in the shower. I felt like crying when this would happen because I just wanted to stop and it was like I physically couldn't until my brain was satisfied that I washed properly a certain way a certain amount of times. Nobody will know, because who sees me in the shower? Nobody. I could crawl into a corner of the bathtub and cry about it as the water broke my skin and nobody would know, and that is a very sad realisation when it comes to OCD. I look at OCD as an invisible illness a lot of the time, because people can't see the obsessions and compulsions. I wish my mind were a projector so I can project my obsessions and compulsions onto a wall so people can see and so I can explain it better.

I had a shelf in my room when I was a teenager, and it was a mess, an organised mess. Things were all over the place because I had a fear of moving them, and things like jewellery boxes or skincare products had to be placed in certain spots. This is known as symmetry or ordering OCD; it becomes uncomfortable when objects are misaligned or not in a certain spot. My brain would throw thoughts at me, like 'Pick up that bottle that dropped and place it on the back of the shelf, or you will get sick and not go to that event you have been waiting for' or 'Someone in your family will die if that bottle isn't put away behind the jewellery box.' As absurd as this sounds, I could not help but believe it. I just couldn't. This is known as magical thinking, like superstition, as if our thoughts had the power to make things happen, things that don't add up in the real world. Numbers, colours, actions, and even words can have the power to cause events to happen or keep them from happening; this is magical thinking in OCD. For me, it was the numbers three, four, and six. Three and six were bad luck as they were related to evil. My mind's OCD made me believe that the number six is related to Satan and evil things happening to me and others around me, the same with the number three because three plus three is six. So, I would avoid doing anything three or six times and buying things in threes or a packet of six. The number four was a good number; it felt good doing things four times or buying four of something if I had to buy more than a couple. If I washed my hands, it was usually four times; if I scrubbed my body in the shower, it would be four times. And if I had to make sure the fridge was closed before I went to bed, I checked it four times. Now to stop this, I had to not give in to the compulsion and check once or not at all. And I did start this exposure therapy, it is called exposure and response prevention (ERP). It consisted of exposing myself to the obsession and compulsion that follow but not doing the compulsion, rather sitting with the fear and discomfort and preventing myself from performing any compulsion. The anxiety will spike and go right up and eventually go back down; this exposure and no response or sometimes delayed response would train my brain to stop doing the compulsions and would start to feel easier with practice and time. When exposure is repeated over time, habituation will start to happen, meaning I will learn that nothing bad is going to happen, and the intensity of the obsession and compulsion will decrease and maybe disappear over time. This is hard work, very hard work, so many individuals suffering from OCD may avoid ERP and throw their arms up in the air and give in because it is so much less frightening and there's so much less suffering. I have, so many times, because it gets overwhelming and the physical symptoms kick in, like increased heart rate, sweating, and fast breathing that I feel I may faint, so I drop the ball and run. This does not mean it is the end of the road, not at all; there are so many more opportunities to tackle OCD with ERP. When done often, it changes your life; it really does. Having fewer obsessions due to ERP is amazing. You feel you have accomplished running a marathon; you feel on top of the world, and so you should. Once an obsession is gone, a huge weight is lifted, and you could scream out from the top of your lungs because it feels that good; it just takes a lot of work, commitment, persistence, and time. It takes courage to do ERP therapy, courage is not the absence of fear, rather the ability to feel the fear and sit with it anyway and continue about your day, telling it, 'I am in control this time, and I will continue my life with or without you here.' Feeling the fear and doing it anyway is courage.

The physical symptoms of OCD range from hot and cold flushes, irritable bowels, acid reflux, abdominal pain and discomfort, diarrhoea, constipation, headaches such as tension headaches, nausea, shaking or trembling, dry mouth. Suffering OCD can appear secretive because a lot of the time, you can't even tell someone has OCD and you don't see them performing their compulsions. The number of times I find myself washing my hands over and over and the skin starts to peel, blister, or become red or raw, I feel, is endless. I didn't like that it gave me a sense of shame, and it was tiring. 'Tap the fridge four times, make sure it's closed before you leave the house,' 'Stare at the stovetop and oven switch for a few seconds to make sure they're off before you go to bed' became part of my daily routine. This was not good because I risked being late to work, even though I never was because of it, thankfully. And me rattling downstairs or walking back and forth annoys my husband, who has to get up early for work; it annoys me too. I just want to go to bed I want to go to sleep because OCD is physically draining. The whole disorder is exhausting; it takes so much out of me. At work, a lot of the days I felt I could curl into a ball in the centre of the room and sleep, but that was frowned upon my management and, let's be honest, not really acceptable. I get asked, 'How can you be tired? You sleep for ten hours.' I don't sleep all the way through, I have nightmares a lot that keep me up, and I have a thousand toilet trips—that's why I am tired.

The Disorders of My Disorder

There are many other disorders associated with OCD; they are part of the OCD package, for example, trichotillomania, a disorder associated with hair pulling. Also, dermatillomania is a disorder associated with skin picking. Now, I am not talking about plucking your eyebrows with tweezers once a month or picking a scab once and never doing it again. No, I am talking about leaving almost no skin around your nails and no hair on your eyelids. These disorders often go hand in hand with OCD. These two picking disorders at times felt out of control. Let us refer to them as picking disorders, because I don't want to be typing the words so many times—they are too long.

Looking back now, I remember as far back as primary school, maybe year four or five, when I started nail biting and biting or picking the skin around the nail. I would get picked on for it, which was horrible; it was very obvious. I try to control it now, but it never really goes away; at times, I bleed from the skin biting and when lemon, salt, or vinegar came on them while in the kitchen or eating, it would burn, and my fingers would swell up. This upset my parents; Mum would look at my fingers and tell me to look at what I'm doing to them with a sad look on her face. There are different reasons for why this behaviour arises, like when one is anxious, worried, or anticipating something. The picking becomes a calming behaviour as well; it provides a sense of control over the anxiety or situation one is in, until you notice you almost have no eyelashes left and you regret it and don't want to show your face in public. If you were to look into trichotillomania, you will see that people suffering from it pick the hair off their scalp. For me it was similar, yet I did not just pick any hair; it was particular hair around a scab on the middle of my head. I would pick at this scab, not knowing where it came from, but I would pick at it until it was raw and bleeding, until I needed a tissue. This scab on my head was there for such a long time, I'd say months; it would disappear then reappear. I would pick at it; I wanted it gone, yet picking at it gave me some sort of relief. I do find myself picking and biting particularly when I am extremely anxious and when the OCD is screaming at me. We can see that OCD can torture the mind and that it also tortures the body.

OCD does not have one face; it has many. OCD is a disorder within many disorders. I mentioned trichotillomania and dermatillomania; they are disorders within the OCD disorder, and now I will mention eating disorders. If you open my wardrobe, you will notice a fluctuation of sizes, clothes ranging from a size eight to a size twelve. When I first started taking medication for the anxiety and OCD, I dramatically dropped in weight. I was in high school, and I remember all of a sudden being so thin that my school pant would keep sliding down and I had to roll them up at the waist or hold them up while I walked. The pant was so noticeably big that I remember a student saying as I walked through the school hallway, 'Look how much weight she has lost.' A part of me believes the medication may have caused this change, and I also believe it may have been an eating disorder showing its face. My anxiety kept me from eating at school most days, so I would go the whole eight hours or so without food, and if I wanted something from the canteen, I would ask someone to kindly go for me. I would give them money and beg them to buy for me, as I was just too anxious to make the trip. I still remember the taste of a plain buttered bread roll or a spicy beef burger. For years, I kept this up, and when I got home, I would eat dinner like I had not eaten in years. I began to like this weight loss; Mum's friend asked Mum if I was sick or something and losing weight because of that. Mum reassured her I was not sick. Between my brain and myself, I would say I was unwell, mentally though. Body dysmorphia was something that would visit my mind; no matter how slim I was, it was not enough, and I kept finding parts of my body that were big and needed to go. Every time I looked in the mirror, I saw big; it was not until I put the weight back on and looked at the photos of me when I was anorexic that I realised how slim I was. For someone who loves food and enjoys eating, even cooking, I sure had a bad relationship with food. I would deprive or starve myself and over-exercise. I enjoyed parts of that, although I hated it. I would miss out on so many desserts at occasions like birthdays or weekends with family and torture myself by not having any. This at times led to binging. I would get home and eat all the chocolate in sight. Soon after this, I realised I could not go on like this and allowed myself to have treats like chocolate several times a week and just kept it in moderation, then the binging disappeared. I put all the weight back on. I did not become overweight; I was at a healthy weight, the weight most people wanted me to be and even I wanted to be at one point, because I would get upset at how I couldn't fit into any of my dresses—they were all too big. Most things I wanted to wear were too big. I heard someone once say that once you develop an eating disorder, it never really goes away, just like OCD. For me, that is true; it never really does. It often comes to my mind, and I find myself cutting back on food or exercising more than usual. The exercising part was not entirely to stay slim or skinny. It also gave me a sense of control, strength, and time off from my OCD. When I am in the gym, I feel at peace and in a good space. Yes, OCD would kick in and start to tell me to do this again and that set again, or I didn't do that properly do that again and again. Not all the time though—I was calm and felt good most times.

Looking back at certain times or events of my life makes me feel I may have borderline personality disorder (BPD). It is not uncommon to suffer from several disorders at once; a lot of them link, and symptoms of one disorder could also be symptoms of another, making it difficult to pinpoint what exactly you have! With mental disorders, unlike a physical illness or injury, you can't point to where it hurts or where it is broken and give it a name, fix it, and be done, then move on. You can't see a mental disorder; although they have their physical symptoms, it's not like you can shine a torch onto your forehead and show people where the damage is. This makes it hard to diagnose at times and treat. I explained to my psychiatrist that I feel I may also have BPD; he asked me why and what symptoms I was experiencing. I explained the mood changes, fear of abandonment, and looking back, I saw manipulation, impulsivity, and impaired social relationships. He did agree to an extent and concluded I may fall under the BPD umbrella. This scared me a little bit and brought on feelings of shame again, yet we could both see that OCD is dominant, and we focus on that.

Have you heard of the term *empath*?

I know I am an empath and I can just feel it. I just know. I have always been the sensitive type; by that, I mean really sensitive to people and their emotions. I just pick up on so much that most people probably wouldn't pick up on. Now if you pick up your phone and you Google *empath*, you will read the definition 'a person with the paranormal ability to perceive or read the mental or emotional state of another person'. Well, it is, kind of. Mum and Dad have always described me as sensitive, and when I had certain dreams, Mum and Dad would know. I would share with them. They looked at the dreams as either omens or premonitions, and a lot of the times, they were one of the two. My dreams need a book for themselves. I do feel the dreams are part of being an empath.

I have always picked up on vibes from people. They could be saying something like 'I love you' and I could somehow know if it is true or not. I just know from their eyes from the movement of their facial muscles, and I just sense what they really feel. When someone walks into a room, I can always sense what they feel and what they are likely thinking, and most of the time, it would prove to be true; that person would later say how they felt, and it would be exactly how I thought and described. So, I don't like being lied to because I feel and pick up on that lie like it was a slap in the face. I just feel I over-feel; I feel everything to an extreme. This can be annoying and overwhelming at times. It's almost like a sixth sense, an ability to absorb or feel everybody's emotion, and I honestly find it hard to explain. I suggest you Google it; otherwise, I will go on forever about it.

I mentioned high-functioning anxiety right at the start of the book, and I would say I am high functioning because high-functioning anxiety sufferers seem absolutely fine on the outside; they seem like the perfect hard-working, driven, and successful citizen. Yet little do people know of the turmoil on the inside. That's what high functioning is. We look like our lives are all together, and we are never late to work or take sick days off. We are so reliable and high achievers in all we do. All this is us being afraid to go off the rails, to be less than perfect, to expose our anxiety and suffering, and to be judged.

Have you ever watched the same movie over and over and over again and look forward to watching it again and again? I feel you; hyperfixation is something I do. I become completely immersed in a movie or song, and I watch or listen so many times; this helps me cope with my mental illness. There is a particular movie that I enjoy watching and is on my mind a lot, and particular sings too; they just help me gain a sense of calm and familiarity, a sense of order, and a break from my thoughts. When I hyperfixate on something, I don't just watch it. I analyse it, learn what line comes next, and even feel a sense of closeness to the characters, as if I know them and they are my friends. Sometimes I wonder if my hobbies and interests are all a part of hyperfixation, because when I have an interest or hobby, I will give it my all and do it as much as I can and even progress in such a short period of time because I practice that much. When I practice, my anxiety and obsessions quieten down, and that becomes addictive. I then seek that feeling again and again, so I go back to my hobby.

I wonder if I hyperfixate on people, and that leads to me pushing them away unintentionally, because there was a time when I would over-love and be so needy or demanding that it has driven people away. My insecurities and obsessions can turn relationships sour very quickly and that has happened to me before; my OCD has pushed people away. The constant texting every half hour to see if the other person is okay because my mind would tell me they are in a car accident and to check on them as a compulsion, wanting to be with them all the time, and crying for attention all played a part in a vicious cycle of obsessions and compulsions. Now that I am older, I wish it was different and I wish I knew then what I know now, but that time has gone, and it is in the past. To those people, I am sorry for any heartache or misery my OCD has caused. I don't want to wallow in the past, as tempting as it is.

Learning to Ride the Waves

OCD will always be a part of me. I have learnt to accept that. A huge part of me wishes it won't be and that soon, all this will be over, or one day, I will wake up and this will all be a dream. I will wake up, and Mum and Dad will be next to me, reassuring me it is all okay and that I just had a long nap. Wouldn't that be good? The reality is that probably won't happen. OCD will continue to come at me in waves: small waves, big waves, tidal waves. It will come at me and swallow me whole. When it is ready and hewed me up enough, it will spit me out onto shore to recover for a little bit before swallowing me up again. If I can learn to ride the waves, it may not be so bad. With the help of medication and therapy, I am riding some of the waves, just not all. If you are reading this and you are in the same boat, please know that I know it is so hard and such a dark space to be in.

Being a slow metaboliser is rare, I have had my doctor tell me it is very rare and I am special, so if you don't have that and reading about it is all new, I am glad you now know because you could help someone some day that is suffering and is struggling to find the right medication or dosage. Writing this book was something I feel I had to do like a rite of passage. Thank you taking the time to read it. It was not easy to write, and as an introvert, I could crawl away and hide after writing and sharing this. I will continue to be me in my OCD and all its glory; I don't really have a choice. I will continue therapy, ride the waves, and expose myself to my fears without running from them. Acceptance and sitting with the fears are what you are supposed to do to win over OCD. As they say, get comfortable with being uncomfortable.

If you have read this book to find hope, support, and answers, I hope you have. I know how scary it can be. I know how sad it can get. Make all the art you like and write and sing all the songs you want to express yourself and what you are going through if that is what you enjoy doing. I now see why it is called the doubting disease. Because it is the fear of the unknown, the what-ifs, the maybes, the 'I could have' and 'should I?', the not being able to handle not knowing if something is right or wrong. Is the fridge closed? Is my house on fire? Did I turn off the stove? Did I leave the tap running?

Did I tap this and that enough times? This tortures my mind, and I live in agonising doubt. I have to let it be, knowing or not knowing acceptance is key.

If you are a parent reading this, please pay attention to your children in every way, because too often in life, we think we are paying all the attention in the world and doing the right thing for them when we are actually not, and all these silent screams for help go unnoticed. As an adult, I wish I had the help back when I was a child. I wish I were taken under the wing of someone who was able to help me and could help me. I just wonder how different things would have been if that did happen. The access to healthcare and support for children and their families these days is so different from twenty or thirty-plus years ago. Mental illness used to be looked at as taboo, and having a mental illness made you crazy. Families would just not talk about it or keep it secret because of the negative stigma in the world. These children who had no help back then have to carry a heavy burden as adults and suffer so much longer than they need to; their lives are robbed of joy and peace because they weren't given the help they needed. So please don't disregard what you think may be or if your child is showing symptoms; there is absolutely no shame in getting help, but there is shame in turning a blind eye. I work with children; this is a passion of mine, and I look forward to shaping the minds of our future and celebrating each child for their unique self, but too often, I see families turning away from help and the advice from professionals and the people who work closely with their child. Get them the help they need and deserve so they bloom and become adults who have the tools and resources to help themselves and manage.

I will end by encouraging you to read the poem 'Desiderata' by Max Ehrmann. I hold this poem close to my heart. It is words I live by and words that help me find peace in the confusion of life; it may help you find your peace. Seek the things that provide light in your darkest hours, peace in all the noise, and hope in all the confusion and then share that light that you find.